SEASONS OF GROWTH

GROUP DIRECTORY

Pass this Directory around and have your Group Members
fill in their names and phone numbers

Name

Phone

_____   _____

_____   _____

_____   _____

_____   _____

_____   _____

_____   _____

_____   _____

_____   _____

_____   _____

_____   _____

_____   _____

_____   _____

_____   _____

_____   _____

SEASONS OF GROWTH

EDITING AND PRODUCTION TEAM:

James F. Couch, Jr., Lyman Coleman, Sharon Penington, Cathy Tardif,
Christopher Werner, Matthew Lockhart, Erika Tiepel,
Richard Peace, Andrew Sloan, Scott Lee

NASHVILLE, TENNESSEE

Seasons of Growth - Marriage
© 1988, 1998, 2003 Serendipity House
Reprinted July 2004

Published by Serendipity House Publishers
Nashville, Tennessee

ISBN: 1-5749-4302-2

Dewey Decimal Classification: 306.81
Subject Heading: MARRIAGE

Unless otherwise indicated, Scripture quotations are taken from the
Holman Christian Standard Bible®,
Copyright © 1999, 2000, 2002, 2003 by Holman Bible Publishers.
Used by permission.

Scripture quotations marked (NIV) are taken from *The Holy Bible, New International Version®. NIV®.* Copyright © 1973, 1978, 1984 by International Bible Society. Used by permission of Zondervan Publishing House. All rights reserved.

To purchase additional copies of this resource or other studies:
ORDER ONLINE at www.SerendipityHouse.com
WRITE Serendipity House, 117 10th Avenue North, Nashville, TN 37234
FAX (615) 277-8181
PHONE (800) 525-9563

1-800-525-9563
www.SerendipityHouse.com

Printed in the United States of America
10 09 08 07 06 05 04   2 3 4 5 6 7 8 9 10

TABLE OF CONTENTS

SESSION	REFERENCE	SUBJECT	PAGE
1	John 2:1–11	Beginnings	15
2	James 1:2–12	For Better or Worse	23
3	Genesis 2:18–25	Love, Honor, Cherish	31
4	John 13:1–17	Please Pass the Roles	37
5	Luke 2:41–52	Baby Makes Three	45
6	Song of Songs 1:16 2:1–7; 4:1–7	One Flesh	51
7	1 Corinthians 13:1–7	Till Death Do Us Part	57

CORE VALUES

Community: The purpose of this curriculum is to build community within the body of believers around Jesus Christ.

Group Process: To build community, the curriculum must be designed to take a group through a step-by-step process of sharing your story with one another.

Interactive Bible Study: To share your "story," the approach to Scripture in the curriculum needs to be open-ended and right brain—to "level the playing field" and encourage everyone to share.

Developmental Stages: To provide a healthy program throughout the four stages of the life cycle of a group, the curriculum needs to offer courses on three levels of commitment: (1) Beginner Level—low-level entry, high structure, to level the playing field; (2) Growth Level—deeper Bible study, flexible structure, to encourage group accountability; (3) Discipleship Level—in-depth Bible study, open structure, to move the group into high gear.

Target Audiences: To build community throughout the culture of the church, the curriculum needs to be flexible, adaptable and transferable into the structure of the average church.

Mission: To expand the Kingdom of God one person at a time by filling the "empty chair." (We add an extra chair to each group session to remind us of our mission.)

INTRODUCTION

Each healthy small group will move through various stages as it matures.

STAGE ONE

Birth Stage: This is the time in which group members form relationships and begin to develop community. The group will spend more time in icebreaker exercises, relational Bible study and covenant building.

STAGE FOUR

Multiply Stage: The group begins the multiplication process. Members pray about their involvement in new groups. The "new" groups begin the life cycle again with the Birth Stage.

STAGE TWO

Growth Stage: Here the group begins to care for one another as it learns to apply what they learn through Bible study, worship and prayer.

STAGE THREE

Develop Stage: The inductive Bible study deepens while the group members discover and develop gifts and skills. The group explores ways to invite their neighbors and coworkers to group meetings.

Subgrouping: If you have nine or more people at a meeting, Serendipity recommends you divide into subgroups of 3–6 for the Bible study. Ask one person to be the leader of each subgroup and to follow the directions for the Bible study. After 30 minutes, the Group Leader will call "time" and ask all subgroups to come together for the Caring Time.

Each group meeting should include all parts of the "three-part agenda."

Ice-Breaker: Fun, history-giving questions are designed to warm the group and to build understanding about the other group members. You can choose to use all of the Ice-Breaker questions, especially if there is a new group member that will need help in feeling comfortable with the group.

One of the purposes of this book is to begin a group. Therefore, getting to know one another and bonding together are essential to the success of this course. The goal is to get acquainted during the Ice-Breaker part of each group session.

Bible Study: The heart of each meeting is the reading and examination of the Bible. The questions are open, discover questions that lead to further inquiry. Reference notes are provided to give everyone a "level playing field." The emphasis is on understanding what the Bible says and applying the truth to real life. The questions for each session build. There is always at least one "going deeper" question provided. You should always leave time for the last of the "questions for interaction." Should you choose, you can use the optional "going deeper" question to satisfy the desire for the challenging questions in groups that have been together for a while.

To help bond together as a group, it is important for everyone to participate in the Bible Study. There are no right or wrong answers to the questions. The group members should strive to make all of the other group members feel comfortable during the Bible Study time. Because we all have differing levels of biblical knowledge, it is essential that we appreciate the personal context from which answers are given. We don't have to know much about Scripture to bring our own perspectives on the truths contained in the Scriptures. It is vital to keep encouraging all group members to share what they are observing as we work through these important Bible passages.

Caring Time: All study should point us to actions. Each session ends with prayer and direction in caring for the needs of the group members. You can choose between several questions. You should always pray for the "empty chair." Who do you know that could fill that void in your group?

Small groups help the larger body of Christ in many ways: caring for individuals, holding one another up in prayer, providing emotional support and in bringing new people into the body through filling the empty chair. Each week it is important to remember to pray for those who God would bring to fill your empty chair.

SHARING YOUR STORY: These sessions are designed for members to share a little of their personal lives each time. Through a number of special techniques, each member is encouraged to move from low risk, less personal sharing to higher risk responses. This helps develop the sense of community and facilitates caregiving.

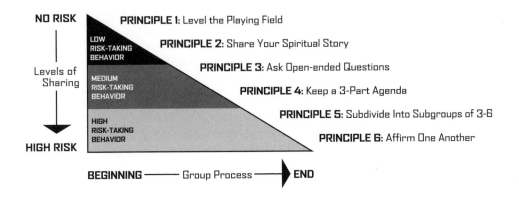

GROUP COVENANT: A group covenant is a "contract" that spells out your expectations and the ground rules for your group. It's very important that your group discuss these goals—preferably as part of the first session.

GROUND RULES:

- **Priority:** While you are in the group, you give the group meeting priority.

- **Participation:** Everyone participates and no one dominates.

- **Respect:** Everyone is given the right to their own opinion and all questions are encouraged and respected.

- **Confidentiality:** Anything that is said in the meeting is never repeated outside the meeting.

- **Empty Chair:** The group stays open to new people at every meeting.

- **Support:** Permission is given to call upon each other in time of need—even in the middle of the night.

- **Advice Giving:** Unsolicited advice is not allowed.

- **Mission:** We agree to do everything in our power to start a new group as our mission.

GOALS:

- The time and place this group is going to meet is _____.

- Responsibility for refreshments is _____.

- Child care is _____ responsibility.

- This group will meet until _____ at which time we will decide to split into new groups or continue our sessions together.

- Our primary purpose for meeting is: _____.

OUR SMALL GROUP COVENANT

1. The facilitator for this group is _____.

2. The apprentice facilitator for this group is _____.

3. This group will meet from _____ to _____ on _____.

4. This group will normally meet at _____.

5. Child care will be arranged by _____.

6. Refreshments will be coordinated by _____.

7. Our primary purpose for meeting is _____.

8. Our secondary purpose for meeting is _____.

9. We all agree to follow the ground rules listed below:

   a. This meeting will be given priority in our schedules.

   b. Everyone will participate in each meeting and no one will dominate a meeting.

   c. Each has a right to one's own opinion and all questions will be respected.

   d. Everything that is said in group meetings is never to be repeated outside of the meeting.

   e. This group will be open to new people at every meeting.

   f. Permission is given for all to call on each other in time of need.

   g. Unsolicited advice is not allowed.

   h. We agree to fill the empty chair and work toward starting new groups.

10. We are to hold one another accountable to meet any commitments mutually agreed upon by this group.

I agree to all of the above _____ date _____

INDIVIDUAL AND GROUP NEEDS SURVEY

Check the types of studies that you find most interesting:
- ○ Issues about spiritual development, such as learning to love like God does or knowing God's will.
- ○ Studying about the life and message of Jesus Christ.
- ○ Issues about personal development, such as managing stress or understanding the stages of growth in marriage.
- ○ Learning about the major truths of the Christian faith.
- ○ Studying the teaching of the Apostle Paul.
- ○ Working through specific areas of personal struggle, such as coping with teenagers or recovering from divorce.
- ○ Learning about the books of the New Testament other than the Gospels and Epistles of Paul.

Rank the following factor in order of importance to you with 1 being the highest and five being the lowest:
- _____ The passage of Scripture that is being studied.
- _____ The topic or issue that is being discussed.
- _____ The affinity of group members (age, vocation, interest).
- _____ The mission of the group (service projects, evangelism, starting groups).
- _____ Personal encouragement.

Rank the following spiritual development needs in order of interest to you with 1 being the highest and 5 being the lowest:
- _____ Learning how to become a follower of Christ.
- _____ Gaining a basic understanding of the truths of the faith.
- _____ Improving my disciplines of devotion, prayer, reading Scripture.
- _____ Gaining a better knowledge of what is in the Bible.
- _____ Applying the truths of Scripture to my life.

Of the various studies listed below check the appropriate boxes to indicate:
P - if you would be interested in studying this for your **personal needs**
G - if you think it would be helpful for your **group**
F - if **friends** that are not in the group would come to a group studying this subject

Growing in Christ Series (7-week studies)	P	G	F
Keeping Your Cool: Dealing with Stress	○	○	○
Personal Audit: Assessing Your life	○	○	○
Seasons of Growth: Stages of Marriage	○	○	○
Checking Your Moral Compass: Personal Morals	○	○	○
Women of Faith (8 weeks)	○	○	○
Men of Faith	○	○	○
Being Single and the Spiritual Quest	○	○	○

Foundations of the Faith (7-week studies)

	P	G	F
Knowing Jesus	O	O	O
Foundational Truths	O	O	O
God and the Journey to Truth	O	O	O
The Christian in the Postmodern World	O	O	O

Fellowship Church Series (6-week studies)

	P	G	F
Wired for Worship (worship as a lifestyle)	O	O	O
X-Trials: Takin' Life to the X-treme (James)	O	O	O
Virtuous Reality: The Relationships of David	O	O	O
Praying for Keeps (life of prayer)	O	O	O
Character Tour (developing godly character)	O	O	O

Becoming a Disciple (7-week studies)

	P	G	F
Discovering God's Will	O	O	O
Time for a Checkup	O	O	O
Learning to Love	O	O	O
Making Great Kids	O	O	O
Becoming Small-Group Leaders	O	O	O

Understanding the Savior (13-week studies)

	P	G	F
Jesus, the Early Years (Mark 1 – 8)	O	O	O
Jesus, the Final Days (Mark 9 – 16)	O	O	O
John: God in the Flesh (John 1 – 11)	O	O	O
John: The Passion of the Son (John 12 – 21)	O	O	O
The Life of Christ	O	O	O
Sermon on the Mount: Jesus, the Teacher	O	O	O
The Parables of Jesus	O	O	O
The Miracles of Jesus	O	O	O

The Message of Paul

	P	G	F
Who We Really Are: Romans 1 – 7 (13 weeks)	O	O	O
Being a Part of God's Plan: Romans 8 – 16 (13 weeks)	O	O	O
Taking on Tough Issues: 1 Corinthians (13 weeks)	O	O	O
Living by Grace: Galatians (13 weeks)	O	O	O
Together in Christ: Ephesians (12 weeks)	O	O	O
Running the Race: Philippians (7 weeks)	O	O	O
Passing the Torch: 1 & 2 Timothy (13 weeks)	O	O	O

Men of Purpose Series (13-week studies geared to men)

	P	G	F
Overcoming Adversity: Insights into the Life of Joseph	O	O	O
Fearless Leadership: Insights into the Life of Joshua	O	O	O
Unwavering Tenacity: Insights into the Life of Elijah	O	O	O
Shoulder to Shoulder: Insights into the Life of the Apostles	O	O	O

Words of Faith

	P	G	F
The Church on Fire: Acts 1 – 14 (13 weeks)	O	O	O
The Irrepressible Witness: Acts 15 – 28 (13 weeks)	O	O	O
The True Messiah: Hebrews (13 weeks)	O	O	O
Faith at Work: James (12 weeks)	O	O	O
Staying the Course: 1 Peter (10 weeks)	O	O	O
Walking in the Light: 1 John (11 weeks)	O	O	O
The End of Time: Revelation 1 – 12 (13 weeks)	O	O	O
The New Jerusalem: Revelation 13 – 22 (13 weeks)	O	O	O

301 Bible Studies with Home Work Assignments (13-weeks)

	P	G	F
Life of Christ: Behold the Man	O	O	O
Sermon on the Mount: Examining Your Life	O	O	O
Parables: Virtual Reality	O	O	O
Miracles: Signs and Wonders	O	O	O
Ephesians: Our Riches in Christ	O	O	O
Philippians: Joy under Stress	O	O	O
James: Walking the Talk	O	O	O
1 John: The Test of Faith	O	O	O

Life Connections Series (*Unique series blends master-teacher larger group format with effective small-group encounters; 13-week studies*)

	P	G	F
Essential Truth: Knowing Christ Personally	O	O	O
Vital Pursuits: Developing My Spiritual Life	O	O	O
Authentic Relationships: Being Real in an Artificial World	O	O	O
Unique Design: Connecting with the Christian Community	O	O	O
Acts: Model for Today's Church	O	O	O
Critical Decisions: Surviving in Today's World	O	O	O
Colossians: Navigating Successfully Through Cultural Chaos	O	O	O
Intentional Choices: Discovering Contentment in Stressful Times	O	O	O
Unleashed Influence: Power of servant Leadership	O	O	O

Felt Need Series (7-week studies)

	P	G	F
Stress Management: Finding the Balance	O	O	O
12 Steps: The Path to Wholeness	O	O	O
Divorce Recovery: Picking Up the Pieces	O	O	O
Parenting Adolescents: Easing the Way to Adulthood	O	O	O
Blended Families: Yours, Mine, Ours	O	O	O
Healthy Relationships: Living Within Defined Boundaries	O	O	O
Marriage Enrichment: Making a Good Marriage Better	O	O	O

For the latest studies visit www.SerendipityHouse.com or call 1-800-525-9563.

Session 1
BEGINNINGS

Scripture John 2:1–11

 Welcome to this course for couples who want to make a good marriage better. Too often people pay attention to their marriage only when a serious problem develops. That is like taking your car in only when it needs to be repaired, but never for maintenance. Certainly marriage is much more valuable than a car.

Paying attention to the marriage relationship means taking time to celebrate the good and to learn from the bad. It means talking about the pressures of marriage—stress from work, finances, schedules, in-laws, children and grandchildren.

These pressures would be easier to handle if it weren't for the fact that we also have to adapt to each other. As soon as we think we have the other person figured out, he or she changes, and we have to readapt. Still, it is such growth and change that can bring excitement (as well as challenge) to a marriage.

In this course, we will discuss many areas where growth can occur. We will take time to look at our differing values and how they can enrich marriage; the extended family relationships that both enhance and challenge our union. We will look at the beauty and excitement our sexuality brings to marriage. Finally, we will focus on the challenge of that part of the vows that says: "till death do us part."

Every session in this course has three parts: (1) **Ice-Breaker**—to get to know each other better and introduce the topic, (2) **Bible Study**—to share your life through a passage of Scripture, and (3) **Caring Time**—to share prayer concerns and pray for one another.

Ice-Breaker : 15 min.
CONNECT WITH YOUR GROUP

Leader
Be sure to read the introductory material in the front of this book prior to this first session. To help your group members get acquainted, have each person introduce him or herself and then take turns answering the Ice-Breaker questions.

Take turns answering the following questions about your beginnings as a couple. (If your spouse leaves out some of the juicy details, feel free to add to his or her story!)

1. What two adjectives describe your first impression of your spouse?
   ○ Gorgeous.
   ○ Irresistible.
   ○ Handsome.
   ○ Innocent.
   ○ Charming.
   ○ Crazy.
   ○ Fun.
   ○ Spiritual.
   ○ Classy.
   ○ Wild.
   ○ Old-fashioned.
   ○ Other_____.

2. How did you first meet? Where was it? What occasion?

3. Where did you go on your first date? What happened?

4. What was your marriage proposal like? (Include where and how.)

Bible Study : 30 min.
READ SCRIPTURE + DISCUSS

This Bible story is about a wedding in Cana where Jesus performed his first miracle by turning water into wine. Weddings in Jesus' time were important events. Relatives and townspeople would gather to celebrate, often for up to a week! To run out of wine would have been a great social embarrassment. Read John 2:1–11 and note how the disciples react to Jesus.

Jesus Changes Water to Wine

John: *On the third day a wedding took place in Cana of Galilee. Jesus' mother was there, and ²Jesus and His disciples were invited to the wedding as well. ³When the wine ran out, Jesus' mother told Him,*

Mary: *"They don't have any wine."*

Jesus: *⁴"What has this concern of yours to do with Me, woman?" Jesus asked. "My hour has not yet come."*

Mary: *⁵"Do whatever He tells you," His mother told the servants.*

John: *⁶Now six stone water jars had been set there for Jewish purification. Each contained 20 or 30 gallons.*

Jesus: *⁷"Fill the jars with water," Jesus told them.*

John:	*So they filled them to the brim. ⁸Then He said to them,*
Jesus:	*"Now draw some out and take it to the chief servant."*
John:	*And they did. ⁹When the chief servant tasted the water (after it had become wine), he did not know where it came from—though the servants who had drawn the water knew. He called the groom ¹⁰and told him,*
Chief Servant:	*"Everybody sets out the fine wine first, then, after people have drunk freely, the inferior. But you have kept the fine wine until now."*
John:	*¹¹Jesus performed this first sign in Cana of Galilee. He displayed His glory, and His disciples believed in Him.*

John 2:1–11

 # QUESTIONS FOR INTERACTION

Leader
Refer to the Study Notes at the conclusion of this session as needed. If 30 minutes is not enough time to answer all of the questions in this section, conclude the Bible Study by answering question 7.

1. What is the funniest thing that happened at your wedding?

2. How would you compare the way Jesus' mother acted at the wedding to the way your parents acted at your wedding?

○ My mother acted just like Jesus' mother.
○ My dad cried when he gave me away.
○ Everything went fine, until …
○ I don't even want to talk about it.
○ Other_____.

3. Why do you think Jesus chose this event for his first miracle?

4. What does verse 11 say was the end result of this miracle?

5. What is meant by the word "sign" to describe this miracle? What "signs" of God's presence have you seen in your life?

6. In what ways has Jesus "turned water into wine" in your marriage—taken something ordinary and turned it into something special?

7. How would you compare the "wine level" (zest for love and life) of your marriage today to that of the day you were married?
    ○ Well …
    ○ It's different.
    ○ We've grown.
    ○ We've settled down.
    ○ The cork has been out of the wine bottle for a while.
    ○ It's much better now.
    ○ Other_____.

 GOING DEEPER:
If your group has time and/or wants a challenge, go on to this question.

8. What "sign" or miracle would bring you spiritually closer as a couple? How much should faith depend on "signs"?

 Caring Time : 15 min.
APPLY THE LESSON AND PRAY FOR ONE ANOTHER

Leader
Take some extra time in this first session to go over the group covenant found at the beginning of this book. At the close, pass around your books and have everyone sign the Group Directory. You, as leader, pray for the requests shared by the group.

This very important time is for developing and expressing your concern for each other as group members through praying.

1. Agree on the group covenant found in the introductory pages.

2. What miracle would you like to ask Jesus for today? Are you in need of a "sign" to strengthen your faith?

3. Share any other prayer requests and then close in prayer. Pray specifically for God to lead you to another couple to bring next week to fill the empty chair(s) (see the introductory pages).

 ## NEXT WEEK

Today we considered the wedding at Cana, where Jesus performed his first miracle. Jesus brought great joy into this couple's marriage through the turning of water into wine. In the coming week, together as a couple, pray and ask Jesus for help in making your marriage better. Next week we will talk about handling the difficult times of marriage.

 ## NOTES ON JOHN 2:1–11

Summary: This is the first recorded miracle of Jesus. He shows his mastery over the physical world and reveals his power to his disciples and his mother. We see both his human responsibility toward his mother and his single-mindedness as Son of God.

2:1 On the third day. This phrase begs us to read this story in light of the reality of Jesus' resurrection on the third day after his death. The story highlights both the new quality of life brought through Jesus' death and resurrection, and his intention to replace the formal religious structures of his day with joyful intimacy with God. **a wedding took place**. A wedding was a week-long feast in which much wine was consumed. Jesus' presence here reminds us that he was not an ascetic who avoided the celebrations of life. **in**

Cana. The exact location of this village is unknown, but it is believed to have been near Nazareth.

2:2 Jesus and His disciples. According to John's chronology thus far, Jesus only has five disciples, all residents of the immediate area (1:35,40-41,43-49).

2:3 When the wine ran out. This was a humiliating social situation. It would imply that the host was someone too miserly to provide adequate refreshments for the guests. **Jesus' mother**. Mary plays a minor role in this

Gospel, appearing only here and in 19:25. Her concern for the situation as well as her relationship to the servants (v. 5) indicates she may have been active in the planning of the wedding. **They don't have any wine.** Why Jesus' mother approached Jesus with this concern is unknown, since Jesus had not previously done anything to make her expect that he could solve the problem. It implies her awareness of his divine power.

2:4 What has this concern of yours to do with me, woman? Since the time for his messianic role is at hand, Jesus is making it clear that from now on that there are other loyalties and relationships. **My hour.** Jesus' response communicates that he will operate on the time frame his Father has assigned him.

2:5 Do whatever He tells you. Again, the reason for Mary's confidence in pressing on with this concern is unknown. The phrase does show that the initiative is left with Jesus.

2:6 six stone water jars. Although not required by the Law of Moses, many Jews in Jesus' day, practiced purification rituals based on those required of the priests (Ex. 30:19–20; Mark 7:1–4). A large event like this wedding would require a great deal of water for such cleansing. The use of these jars implies that Jesus is replacing the old ways of ritual purification. **20 or 30 gallons.** Drinking wine did not have the associations with alcoholism and alcohol abuse as it does today.

Providing wine was an expression of one's desire that others join in as celebrants at a happy occasion. Jesus' provision of such an ample amount of wine puts him in the place of a host, generously and graciously providing for his guests.

2:9 he did not know where it came from. Throughout John's gospel that the identity of Jesus is revealed only to those he chooses. Others see but do not comprehend.

2:10 Everybody sets out the fine wine first. Typically, the best wine would be served when the guests would be most able to appreciate it. Later on, when they are less likely to notice, a cheaper quality of wine would be introduced.

2:11 sign. John uses this term frequently to describe Jesus' miracles to encourage his readers to see God's presence in Jesus (John 1:12). **glory.** This was the disciples' first glimpse of God's glory manifested in Jesus. The fact that this act involves creative power indicates, "the Word became flesh" (John 1:14). His generous provision of such a great amount of wine and his ability to transform a potentially dismal situation into one of richness and abundance reflects that, "We have all received grace after grace from His fullness" (John 1:16).

Session 2
FOR BETTER OR WORSE

Scripture James 1:2–12

LAST WEEK

In last week's session, we shared some of the ups and downs of our beginnings as couples. We also considered Jesus' first miracle of turning water into wine at a wedding. Through this miracle he added great joy to that couple's celebration, and "He displayed His glory, and His disciples believed in Him" (v. 11). We were reminded that, as Jesus' mother did, we can also turn to Jesus to help bring an abundance of joy into our marriages. This week we will turn our attention to getting through the hard times of marriage.

There are times when things are "worse" instead of "better." Since the time of Adam and Eve, married couples have experienced difficulties and trials. The trials encountered often vary according to the stage of the marriage. After the honeymoon is over, the marriage relationship must become more intentional. In the first years of marriage, couples are getting to know each other. In the middle years, effort must be put into balancing work with raising children. And after the children leave, the marriage enters the mature stage where often the relationship needs to be redefined.

What really makes a marriage succeed? In addition to love, commitment and responsibility are necessary. When the going gets tough, as it does in all marriages, couples need to work hard to keep the union intact. Long-term successful couples never take each other for granted. Even while raising children, they realize that their first and main commitment is to being a couple.

Ice-Breaker : 15 min.
CONNECT WITH YOUR GROUP

Leader

Begin this session with a word of prayer. Have your group members take turns sharing their responses to the Ice-Breaker activity. Be sure that everyone gets a chance to participate.

What are some of the little things in life that drive you crazy? Answer the following questions and see how others react to the little trials of life.

1. Look at the following list and each of you give a rating of 1 ("this doesn't bother me at all") to 10 ("stay out of my way when this happens!") for each item. Then take turns sharing your ratings, and see how your response compares to your spouse's response!

____Someone cuts me off in traffic.

____Someone takes up two parking spaces.

____A telephone solicitor calls during a meal.

____I have my favorite show pre-empted for a news conference.

____A government agency makes me fill out unneeded paper work.

____Someone forgets to replace the toilet paper.

____Someone constantly channel-surfs.

____Your own pet peeve: _____.

2. Describe how you usually react to the frustrations of life. Describe how your spouse normally reacts to frustration.

Bible Study : 30 min.
READ SCRIPTURE + DISCUSS

Leader

Have a member of the group, selected ahead of time, read aloud the Scripture passage. Then divide into subgroups of three to six and discuss the Questions for Interaction.

When James wrote the following passage he was the pastor of a church where there was high unemployment in the region, no welfare system except the church, and many people were on the verge of starvation. With these hard times in mind, James gives some advice on how to cope. Read James 1:2–12 and note the rewards of persevering under trials.

Trials and Temptations

²Consider it a great joy, my brothers, whenever you experience various trials, ³knowing that the testing of your faith produces endurance. ⁴But endurance must do its complete work, so that you may be mature and complete, lacking nothing.

⁵Now if any of you lacks wisdom, he should ask God, who gives to all generously and without criticizing, and it will be given to him. ⁶But let him ask in faith without doubting. For the doubter is like the surging sea, driven and tossed by the wind. ⁷That person should not expect to receive anything from the Lord. ⁸An indecisive man is unstable in all his ways.

⁹The brother of humble circumstances should boast in his exaltation; ¹⁰but the one who is rich should boast in his humiliation, because he will pass away like a flower of the field. ¹¹For the sun rises with its scorching heat and dries up the grass; its flower falls off, and its beautiful appearance is destroyed. In the same way, the rich man will wither away while pursuing his activities.

¹²Blessed is a man who endures trials, because when he passes the test he will receive the crown of life that He has promised to those who love Him.

James 1:2–12

? | QUESTIONS FOR INTERACTION

Leader

Refer to the Study Notes at the end of this session as needed. If 30 minutes is not enough time to answer all of the questions in this section, conclude the Bible Study by answering question 7.

1. In your own marriage, what was the first real crisis you had to face and how did you deal with it?

2. What is the process that James teaches us in verses 3 and 4? How does that work in the marriage relationship?

3. According to James, what should be a Christian's attitude when facing trials? What reward comes with persevering in the faith?

4. Which of the following characteristics do you think are most important in making it through the hard times of a successful marriage? (choose three)
   ○ Integrity.
   ○ Commitment.
   ○ Submission.
   ○ Assertiveness.
   ○ Sense of humor.
   ○ Common sense.
   ○ Love.
   ○ Honesty.
   ○ Flexibility.
   ○ Caring.
   ○ Understanding.
   ○ Patience.
   ○ Being friends.
   ○ Unselfishness.
   ○ Other_____.

5. In what ways have the hard times in your marriage brought you closer together?

6. In what ways have the hard times in your marriage brought you closer to God?

7. What is the key verse in this passage for you? How will you apply it to your marriage?

 ## GOING DEEPER:
If your group has time and/or wants a challenge, go on to these questions.

---

8. What is so wrong about being "indecisive" (v. 8)? How could this affect the marriage relationship?

9. How does James turn the status of the rich and poor upside down? What does this say about the proper perspective a Christian should have regarding money matters?

Caring Time : 15 min.

APPLY THE LESSON AND PRAY FOR ONE ANOTHER

Come together for a time of prayer now, knowing that God will grant you the wisdom and perseverance you need for any situation. Share your responses to the following questions and then support and encourage one another in prayer.

1. Share something about your spouse for which you are thankful.

2. What characteristic (listed in question 4) do you feel you should work on in the coming week?

3. How do you feel about praying together as a couple? What do you, as a couple, most need to take to God in prayer?

P. S. Add new group members to the Group Directory at the front of this book.

NEXT WEEK

Today we listened to the wise words of James as he gave us a plan for dealing with hardship in our lives and marriages. We were also given some beautiful promises—promises that God will give wisdom generously to all who ask in faith, and the "crown of life" (v. 12) to those who persevere in trials. In the coming week, make a list of any difficulties you are currently going through and pray for wisdom in handling these situations. Keep a record of how God sees you through each difficulty. Next week we will look at what it truly means to love, honor and cherish our spouse.

Summary: James puts all the difficulties of life into perspective. We should rejoice at being able to participate in the struggle of faith. Our testing is a maturity process that produces proven character. Our responsibility is to have faith that doesn't doubt. This is seen in the context of humility before God. Our part in this process is small, for we all will eventually pass on. If we persist, James tells us that there will be rewards.

1:2 Consider it a great joy. Christians ought to view the difficulties of life with enthusiasm, because the outcome of trials will be beneficial. The joy he is talking about is not just a feeling, however. It is a form of activity. It is active acceptance of adversity. **various trials.** The word "trials" has the dual sense of "adversity" (e.g., disease, persecution, tragedy) and "temptations" (e.g., lust, greed, trust in wealth).

1:3 One reason the Christian can rejoice in suffering is because good does come out of the pain. **endurance.** This word is used in the sense of active overcoming rather than passive acceptance.

1:4 do its complete work. Perfection is not automatic—it takes time and effort. **mature and complete.** James has in mind here wholeness of character. He is not calling for some sort of esoteric perfection or sinlessness. Instead, the emphasis is on moral blamelessness. He is thinking of the integrated life, in contrast to the indecisive person of verses 6–8.

1:5 wisdom. This is not just abstract knowledge, but God-given insight that leads to right living. It is the ability to make correct decisions, especially about moral issues, as one is called upon to do during trials.

1:6 James now contrasts the lack of hesitation on God's part to give (v. 5) with the hesitation on people's part to ask (v. 6). Both here and in 4:3, unanswered prayer is connected to the quality of the asking, not to the unwillingness of God to give. **ask in faith.** To be in one mind about God's ability to answer prayer, to be sure that God will hear and act in accord with his superior wisdom.

1:8 indecisive. To be undecided is to be in two minds—to believe and to disbelieve simultaneously.

1:9–11 Poverty is an example of a trial to be endured but so too is wealth, though in quite a different way.

1:9 brother of humble circumstances. This includes people who are poor in a material and social sense, and who are looked down on because they are poor. **boast.** This becomes possible when the poor see beyond immediate circumstances to their new position as children of God. They may be poor in worldly goods, but they are rich beyond imagination since they are children of God, and heirs of the whole world.

1:10 rich. The peril of riches is that people come to trust in wealth as a source of security. It is a mark of indecisiveness to attempt to serve both God and money.

1:12 Blessed. Happy is the person who has withstood all the trials to the end. **endures.** In verse 3, James says testing produces endurance. Here he points out that such endurance brings the reward of blessedness. **endures trials.** Such a person is like metal that has been purged by fire and is purified of all foreign substances. **crown of life.** As with Paul (Rom. 5:1–5) and Peter (1 Peter 1:6–7), James now focuses on the final result of endurance under trial: eternal life. Crowns were worn at weddings and feasts (signify joy); were given to winners of athletic competitions (signify victory); and worn by royalty.

Session 3
LOVE. HONOR. CHERISH

Scripture **Genesis 2:18–25**

 **LAST WEEK**

Surviving the tough times in marriage was our topic of discussion last week. We studied the words of James as he reminded us to seek God's wisdom and persevere in trials. The reward for faith and perseverance will not only be a better marriage, but also "the crown of life that He has promised to those who love Him" (James 1:12). Today we will consider what it means to truly love, honor and cherish our spouse.

Love, honor and cherish are three simple words that express important things we promised to do when we were married. But what do they mean? Are they just nice-sounding words we use when romance is in the air and that we promptly forget when "the rubber hits the road" in the day-to-day issues of marriage?

There are essentially three New Testament words that can be translated into the English word "love." *Eros* means romantic or sexual love. It often focuses on the physical, and does not express the height of what love can be. *Phileo* is what we sometimes call "brotherly love." This kind of love for our spouse as a companion and fellow traveler on life's journey is also important. But beyond this kind of love is *agape,* which is God's love. This love goes beyond our own self-focused need—it's love with no strings attached. We show this love when we stop thinking "50-50" and give of ourselves fully to the other person's needs and to the needs of our marriage.

Certainly love also includes the idea of "honoring" and cherishing" our partner. To "honor" someone is, according to Webster, to show him or her "high regard or respect." To "cherish" our spouse means to "hold them dear"—to value our spouse as more dear to us than professional recognition, material luxury or any of the other things we sometimes place ahead of our marriage.

Ice-Breaker : 15 min.
CONNECT WITH YOUR GROUP

Describe the perfect romantic day with your spouse by finishing the following sentences. In this fantasy, money is no object; so let your imagination run wild. (Share your whole scenario before going on to the next person.)

1. For my perfect romantic day my spouse and I would travel by Lear Jet to ...

2. We would spend the day ...
   ○ In recreational pursuits, like ... .
   ○ Talking and walking hand in hand.
   ○ Playing on the beach.
   ○ Shopping and exploring.
   ○ Meeting new people.
   ○ Other_____.

3. At dinner I would have (singer's name) flown in to sing (a favorite song) just for us.

4. We would top off the evening by ...
   ○ Dancing all night.
   ○ Taking a walk under the stars.
   ○ Going to a special concert.
   ○ "Turning in" early.
   ○ Other_____.

Bible Study : 30 min.
READ SCRIPTURE ÷ DISCUSS

Leader

Have a member of the group, selected ahead of time, read aloud the Scripture passage. Then discuss the Questions for Interaction, breaking up into smaller subgroups as needed.

This part of the creation account focuses on the beginning of human history. Adam is given the responsibility to care for the earth under God's sovereignty, but not alone. In this passage we see God respond to Adam's need for companionship, as he creates woman from man. Read Genesis 2:18–25 and note how God made people to need each other.

Adam and Eve

¹⁸The Lᴏʀᴅ God said, "It is not good for the man to be alone. I will make a helper suitable for him."

¹⁹Now the Lᴏʀᴅ God had formed out of the ground all the beasts of the field and all the birds of the air. He brought them to the man to see what he would name them; and whatever the man called each living creature, that was its name. ²⁰So the man gave names to all the livestock, the birds of the air and all the beasts of the field.

But for Adam no suitable helper was found. ²¹So the Lᴏʀᴅ God caused the man to fall into a deep sleep; and while he was sleeping, he took one of the man's ribs and closed up the place with flesh. ²²Then the Lᴏʀᴅ God made a woman from the rib he had taken out of the man, and he brought her to the man.

²³The man said,

> "This is now bone of my bones
>   and flesh of my flesh;
> she shall be called 'woman,'
>   for she was taken out of man."

²⁴For this reason a man will leave his father and mother and be united to his wife, and they will become one flesh.

²⁵The man and his wife were both naked, and they felt no shame.

Genesis 2:18-25 (NIV)

? | QUESTIONS FOR INTERACTION

Leader

Refer to the Study Notes at the end of this session as needed. If 30 minutes is not enough time to answer all of the questions in this section, conclude the Bible Study by answering question 7.

1. What is your short definition of a good marriage?
   ○ A spiritual team.
   ○ A safe harbor.
   ○ A lifetime of friendship.
   ○ A fun partnership.
   ○ Other_____

2. Which couple do you look up to as a role model for a good marriage?

3. What does this story say to you about the nature of men and women?
   ○ Men and women need each other.
   ○ Men and women are created with unique authority and responsibility.
   ○ Men are more task-oriented and women more relational.
   ○ Men and women are more alike than different.
   ○ Other_____.

4. What do you think God meant when he referred to Eve as a "suitable helper" (v. 20)?

5. What have you found is the best way to help each other through this journey of life?

6. Which of the following are you most grateful for in your marriage? Which would you like to focus on for growth?
   ○ Our mutual help and support.
   ○ The companionship we share.
   ○ The sizzle of our romance.
   ○ The intimacy of our relationship.
   ○ Other_____.

7. What is one specific way you can love, honor and cherish your spouse in the coming week?

GOING DEEPER:

If your group has time and/or wants a challenge, go on to these questions.

8. What does it mean emotionally and physically that a husband and wife become "one flesh" (v. 24)?

9. In verse 18 God said, "It is not good for the man to be alone." Why do you think God created us to need each other so and to want to be married?

Caring Time : 15 min.

APPLY THE LESSON AND PRAY FOR ONE ANOTHER

Leader
Begin the Caring Time by having group members take turns sharing responses to all three questions. Be sure to save at least the last five minutes for a time of prayer. Ask for two volunteers to pray, remembering to pray for the empty chair.

A wonderful way to be a "suitable helper" to each other is to pray together. Begin by sharing your responses to the following questions. Be sure to offer any prayer requests and concerns before closing in prayer.

1. What was the best thing that happened to you as a couple this past week? What was the worst?

2. In what areas of life would you like to be more united with your spouse?

3. How do you need God's help in creating a more loving and nurturing marriage relationship?

NEXT WEEK

Today we focused on what it means to love, honor and cherish our spouse. We looked at the creation story and saw how God felt Adam's loneliness and his need for a companion. He then created Eve from Adam's rib and united them as one flesh. We were reminded that God created us to find great fulfillment in the marriage relationship. In the coming week, pray for your spouse daily and make an extra effort to do something special that shows your love and appreciation for him or her. Next week we will turn our attention to the different roles that men and women play in marriage, and what it means to serve one another.

 ## NOTES ON GENESIS 2:18-25

Summary: In the beginning Adam and then Eve were in an ideal environment. Adam was given responsibility over the animals and was in close contact with God. To meet the important need for companionship Eve was provided. We can see a relationship of mutual need and trust. Life was peaceful, and they had no shame or fear. Here is a picture of what couples should aim for in marriage. Of course, Adam and Eve at this point were not dealing with a fallen nature. Sin and the cares of world make it difficult. God intended that a man and woman should leave behind their past and step into a union that will bind them together in a loving and supporting relationship.

2:18 It is not good for the man to be alone. God made people to need each other. One of the reasons is the practical matter of procreation. God is a creative God; he created the plants with seeds to procreate. He created a man and then a woman to bring children into the world.

2:20 the man gave names to all the livestock. This was Adam's first act of stewardship over the earth—naming the animals. First, God had named the elements: the sun, the moon, the sky and the land. Then God allowed Adam to name the living creatures.

2:24 leave ... and be united. From the beginning of creation God established the order of the family. Just as Eve was made from Adam's own body, so when a couple is married, the two become one. A man leaves his home, the roots from which he came, and he establishes a new life with his new family. Even though polygamy is practiced in the Old Testament, it is clear from this verse that God's plan was for a man and a woman to become one in lifelong service and union.

2:25 no shame. It is difficult to imagine a world with no shame, a completely innocent world. Yet this is the world that God provided for Adam and Eve. This gives a wonderful picture of God's plan for people; a plan that was soon to be ruined by the arrival of sin.

Session 4
PLEASE PASS THE ROLES
Scripture **John 13:1–17**

 LAST WEEK

In last week's session, we considered what it means to love, honor and cherish our spouse. We looked at God's creation of marriage, and we saw how he desires a husband and wife to be united in a special "oneness" that they can share only with each other. We were reminded to love our spouses with *agape* love, a love that is unconditional and gives itself fully to the other person's needs. Today we will consider how it's possible to achieve this unity in spite of the many differences between men and women. This is especially true when it comes to the roles we play in the marriage relationship.

Marriage therapist John Gray writes in his book *Men Are From Mars, Women Are From Venus* that men (Martians) value power, competency, efficiency and achievement, while women (Venusians) value love, communication, beauty and relationships. The question is this: How do we respond to these differences between men and women? Some fight the differences every step of the way.

Women try to make men think and act more like women, and men try to make women think and act more like men. This is when we need to remember the French phrase—*Viva la Difference*. That phrase essentially means, "long live the differences" between men and women. The key, then, is seeing what our spouse values and then appreciating and respecting the fact that we are different. If we were all the same, what would we contribute to each other? What could we bring to the other person to help them to become more complete? Let us turn to the example that Jesus gave us as we seek to find the answers to these questions.

CONNECT WITH YOUR GROUP

Leader

Welcome and introduce new group members. In this Ice-Breaker activity have each member answer all five questions before going on to the next person. Encourage creativity in adding some roles that are not listed.

Every person plays many roles in his or her life. Check all of the roles that apply to you and add a few more of your own. Then answer the following questions that ask how you feel about these roles.

1. I am a ...
    ○ Father.   ○ Mother.
    ○ Brother.   ○ Sister.
    ○ Husband.   ○ Wife.
    ○ Friend.   ○ Pet owner.
    ○ Employee.   ○ Boss.
    ○ Landlord.   ○ Tenant.
    ○ Political activist.   ○ Taxpayer.
    ○ Church member.   ○ Club member.
    ○ Student.   ○ Volunteer.
    ○ Hobbyist.   ○ Homeowner.
    ○ Stepparent.   ○ Stepchild.
    ○ In-law.   ○ Other_____

2. Which of these roles is the most fun?

3. The most challenging?

4. The most rewarding?

5. The most frustrating?

Bible Study : 30 min.
READ SCRIPTURE + DISCUSS

Leader
Have three group members, selected ahead of time, read aloud the Scripture. Ask one person to read the part of John, the narrator; another to read the part of Jesus; and the third to read the part of Peter.

This story occurs during a special meal Jesus ate with his disciples on the night before his death. It was customary for people's dusty, sandaled feet to be washed, usually by the lowest-ranking servant, before a meal was served. Read John 13:1–17 and note how Jesus' example of servanthood can guide us in determining the role that we play as a husband or wife.

Jesus Washes His Disciples' Feet

John:
Before the Passover Festival, Jesus knew that His hour had come to depart from this world to the Father. Having loved His own who were in the world, He loved them to the end.

²Now by the time of supper, the Devil had already put it into the heart of Judas, Simon Iscariot's son, to betray Him. ³Jesus knew that the Father had given everything into His hands, that He had come from God, and that He was going back to God. ⁴So He got up from supper, laid aside His robe, took a towel, and tied it around Himself. ⁵Next, He poured water into a basin and began to wash His disciples' feet and to dry them with the towel tied around Him.

⁶He came to Simon Peter, who asked Him,

Peter:
"Lord, are You going to wash my feet?"

Jesus:
⁷Jesus answered him, "What I'oing you don't understand now, but afterward you will know."

Peter:
⁸"You will never wash my feet—ever!" Peter said.

Jesus:
Jesus replied, "If I don't wash you, you have no part with Me."

Peter:
⁹Simon Peter said to Him, "Lord, not only my feet, but also my hands and my head."

Jesus:
¹⁰"One who has bathed," Jesus told him, "doesn't need to wash anything except his feet, but he is completely clean. You are clean, but not all of you."

John:	[11]*For He knew who would betray Him. This is why He said, "You are not all clean." [12]When Jesus had washed their feet and put on His robe, He reclined again and said to them,*
Jesus:	*"Do you know what I have done for you? [13]You call Me Teacher and Lord. This is well said, for I am. [14]So if I, your Lord and Teacher, have washed your feet, you also ought to wash one another's feet. [15]For I have given you an example that you also should do just as I have done for you. [16]"I assure you: A slave is not greater than his master, and a messenger is not greater than the one who sent him. [17]If you know these things, you are blessed if you do them.*

John 13:1–17

 ## QUESTIONS FOR INTERACTION

Leader

Refer to the Study Notes at the end of this session as needed. If 30 minutes is not enough time to answer all of the questions in this section, conclude the Bible Study by answering question 7.

1. What is your first reaction to this story about footwashing?

2. What would you have done if you had been there and Jesus started to wash your feet?
   - ○ Left the room.
   - ○ Refused to let him.
   - ○ Broken down and cried.
   - ○ Felt honored by his caring act.
   - ○ Sat there—feeling guilty and unworthy.
   - ○ Jumped up and tried to wash his feet.
   - ○ Other_____.

3. Why do you think Jesus washed the disciples' feet?
   - ○ To illustrate his whole mission.
   - ○ To show them what love is all about.
   - ○ To be an example of servanthood.
   - ○ To show them real leadership.
   - ○ Other_____.

4. How does Jesus define the role of someone who follows him in verses 12–17? What role reversals do you see here?

5. How do you think this teaching of Jesus would be accepted by society in general today?

6. What is holding you back from living a life of service like Jesus demonstrated and taught?
   ○ I might be taken advantage of.
   ○ I don't have time.
   ○ I guess I'm too selfish.
   ○ I haven't had many good role models.
   ○ Nothing really – I'm doing my best.
   ○ Other_____.

7. What would it mean to practice footwashing in your marriage relationship?
   ○ To serve my spouse more.
   ○ To let my spouse serve me.
   ○ To listen to my spouse more.
   ○ To be more patient and forgiving.
   ○ To serve with no strings attached.
   ○ To work at sharing unpleasant tasks.
   ○ To show more affection.
   ○ To show more appreciation.
   ○ To do things that aren't "my job."
   ○ Other_____.

 GOING DEEPER:
If your group has time and/or wants a challenge, go on to these questions.

8. Why did Peter react the way he did? What is the meaning behind Jesus' response in verse 10?

9. In what practical ways are submission and love related in a Christian marriage? What part, if any, does "self-love" play in a marriage relationship?

Caring Time : 15 min.
APPLY THE LESSON AND PRAY FOR ONE ANOTHER

Leader
After sharing responses to all three questions and asking for prayer requests, close in a time of group prayer. Have the members complete this sentence in prayer and then you close, "Lord, would you please encourage me this week through _____?"

Serve each other now by taking some time to offer support and encouragement through sharing and prayer. Before closing in prayer, take turns sharing your answers to the following questions.

1. On a scale of 1 (very little) to 10 (all the time), how would you rate the time that you spent this past week in the role of a "servant"? How would you like that rating to be different?

2. If your spouse could minister to your deepest need in the same way that Jesus ministered to the needs of his disciples, how could your spouse show his or her concern?

3. What words of encouragement would you like to hear from Jesus today?

NEXT WEEK

Today we considered the importance at service to our spouses and how this service can bring joy and completeness to a marriage. We looked at the example that Jesus gave as he washed the feet of his disciples and taught them, and us, about the importance of serving others. This attitude of servanthood especially strengthens the marriage relationship, as we focus on our spouse's needs rather than our own. In the coming week, surprise your spouse by some unexpected act of service. Next week we will discuss the impact that children have on a marriage and try to glean some wisdom from Mary and Joseph as they encounter a problem with parenting Jesus.

Summary: Jesus was constantly surprising the disciples. At the very end of his ministry when they have finally figured out that he is the Son of God, Jesus takes on the role of a common servant. Peter is shocked. In his desire to honor Jesus, he misses the point. We are to give of ourselves as our Lord did. We are to serve others and God. Only when we put God and his ministry first can we be truly his.

13:1 Jesus knew. Here and in verses 3 and 11 John emphasizes what Jesus knew. This lays stress on the fact that Jesus was in charge of the events leading to his death (John 10:18). In contrast to the crowds and to the authorities who didn't know him (John 9:29), Jesus is fully aware of his identity and mission. It was in this full awareness of his dignity and power that Jesus washed the disciples' feet (Phil. 2:5–11). **Having loved His own.** This is not to be taken exclusively, as if Jesus loved only those who were part of his elite club. Christ loves all who respond to his love. **who were in the world.** This Gospel contrasts being in the world with being of the world. Being in the world is just a matter of location, while being of the world means to have the world's values, as opposed to the values of God.

13:3 Jesus' self-knowledge was at the heart of his willingness and ability to serve. This verse says that he knew who he was in terms of where he had come from (the Father), where he was going (back to the Father), and what his role was while he was here.

13:4–5 The other Gospels mention that at the Last Supper there was a discussion among the Twelve about who was the greatest (Luke 22:24), so this may have been the motive for Jesus' action. In that context, Jesus identified the greatest as the one who was the servant (Luke 22:25–27).

13:6 Lord, are You going to wash my feet? Peter, recognizing the impropriety of a master washing the servants' feet, protests. The Greek sentence actually reads more like, "You, wash my feet?" Peter is appalled at this breach of normal procedure.

13:7 afterward you will know. This may simply be referring to verse 17, but more likely it refers to the full understanding of Jesus' servanthood that will be made clear after his resurrection.

13:8 If I don't wash you, you have no part with Me. This lifts the meaning of the footwashing to a higher plane than simply that of an object lesson about humility. Although it could not be understood at the time, the image of being "cleansed" by Jesus became a common picture of what it meant to be forgiven of sin (1 John 1:7,9; Rev. 7:14). Jesus' footwashing was a symbol of the spiritual cleansing he would accomplish for his followers through the Cross.

13:10 One who has bathed. Jesus uses the picture of a person who, after washing completely, travels somewhere. Upon arrival, only his feet need be washed to be clean again. You are clean, but not all of you. Literally, "though not all"—which leaves the meaning ambiguous to the hearers. He may mean only that they are literally still not all clean, but the context shows his real intent was to prepare them for his startling announcement in verse 21 that one of them will betray him.

13:13 Teacher and Lord. These titles of respect for a rabbi were commonly used of Jesus throughout this Gospel (1:38; 13:6). Jesus acknowledges that they are appropriate to him; yet, just as he laid aside the pretension of these titles in order to love others, so they should follow his example in expressing love for one another.

13:16 A slave is not greater than his master. If the master serves, how much more should the servants do so? **a messenger.** This is the same word as "apostle," which only occurs here in this Gospel. An apostle was a person sent with the authority to represent the one who sent him. Jesus' followers are to represent his servanthood to others.

Session 5

 BABY MAKES THREE

Scripture **Luke 2:41–52**

 **LAST WEEK**

How do we respond to the differences between men and women and take on roles of service in the marriage relationship? In last week's session, we looked to Jesus' example to help us answer that question. We saw him wash the feet of the disciples and were reminded that the role of servanthood beautifully expresses the love we have for others. When we put the needs of our spouses before our own, it creates an atmosphere of support and caring, instead of competition and strife. Today we will turn our attention to one of the most difficult, yet most rewarding, aspects of marriage—that of parenting.

Many parents feel ambivalent about raising children. The demands of a job or career can place excessive stress and pressure on couples who want to be conscientious in raising their children. In fact, studies have shown that most mothers work because they have to—they feel like they don't have a choice. About half of these working mothers feel cheated because they are missing out on the best years of their children's lives. It is little wonder that many young couples have chosen to have fewer children or no children at all.

Despite the many obstacles in parenting, many families today are thriving. In his book, *Secrets of Strong Families*, Nick Stinnett explains there are six qualities that are consistently found in strong families. They are commitment, appreciation, communication, time together, spiritual health and coping skills. How can we go about developing these characteristics in our own families?

Much of the practical framework for loving, effective parenting comes from the Bible. In our Scripture passage for today, we will see that Mary and Joseph had some typical parenting problems and concerns with Jesus. While Jesus was not really a typical child, we can learn from his parents' actions.

Ice Breaker : 15 min
CONNECT WITH YOUR GROUP

Leader

Be sure that new group members are introduced and welcomed. Have each member take turns sharing his or her responses to the Ice-Breaker activity.

Great American Blush Awards. Imagine your group is in charge of giving an award for the most embarrassing thing a child has done to their parents. Find out who in your group has had a child do one of the following or share an original story that caused you to blush. Share also how you handled the situation. When everyone is done, vote on which situation was the most embarrassing, and grant that couple the "Ruddy" award.

- ○ Your child shared an embarrassing family incident during the children's sermon.
- ○ Your child repeated a less-than-flattering remark you had made about someone.
- ○ Your older child dressed oddly when company came over.
- ○ Your child publicly contradicted your "little while lie."
- ○ Your little daughter lifted her dress during a public function.
- ○ Your little child shouted during a quiet moment of worship, "I have to go potty!"
- ○ Other_____.

Bible Study : 30 min.
READ SCRIPTURE + DISCUSS

Leader

Have a member of the group, selected ahead of time, read aloud the Scripture passage. Then discuss the Questions for Interaction, breaking up into smaller subgroups of three to six.

This story is the only one in the Bible about Jesus between his infancy and adulthood. Jewish pilgrims from outside Jerusalem, such as Jesus' family, generally traveled to and from the Passover celebration in large caravans. Typically, the women and children would be up front while the men and older boys traveled along behind. It would have been easy during the day for Mary and Joseph to each assume that Jesus was with the other parent or with friends. Read Luke 2:41–52 and note how Jesus responds to his parent's worries.

The Boy Jesus at the Temple

⁴¹*Every year His parents traveled to Jerusalem for the Passover Festival.* ⁴²*When He was 12 years old, they went up according to the custom of the festival.* ⁴³*After those days were over, as they were returning, the boy Jesus stayed behind in Jerusalem, but His parents did not know it.* ⁴⁴*Assuming He was in the traveling party, they went a day's journey. Then they began looking for Him among their relatives and friends.* ⁴⁵*When they did not find Him, they returned to Jerusalem to search for Him.* ⁴⁶*After three days, they found Him in the temple complex sitting among the teachers, listening to them and asking them questions.* ⁴⁷*And all those who heard Him were astounded at His understanding and His answers.* ⁴⁸*When His parents saw Him, they were astonished, and His mother said to Him, "Son, why have You treated us like this? Your father and I have been anxiously searching for You."*

⁴⁹*"Why were you searching for Me?" He asked them. "Didn't you know that I must be involved in My Father's interests?"* ⁵⁰*But they did not understand what He said to them.*

⁵¹*Then He went down with them and came to Nazareth, and was obedient to them. His mother kept all these things in her heart.* ⁵²*And Jesus increased in wisdom and stature, and in favor with God and with people.*

Luke 2:41–52

QUESTIONS FOR INTERACTION

Leader

Refer to the Study Notes at the end of this session as needed. If 30 minutes is not enough time to answer all of the questions in this section, conclude the Bible Study by answering questions 6 and 7.

1. Was obeying your parents ever a problem for you? For your children? How do you get your children to mind without losing yours?

2. What do you think of Jesus' parents' behavior in this story?

3. As a parent, how would you have reacted when you finally found Jesus in the temple courts three days later?
    ○ Cried and given him a big hug.
    ○ Yelled and screamed at him
    ○ Felt confused as to what he meant.
    ○ Just felt relieved the incident was over.
    ○ Gently rebuked him, as Mary did.
    ○ Grounded him for 1,589 weeks!
    ○ Listened to his explanation.
    ○ Other_____.

4. Why didn't Mary and Joseph understand what Jesus was saying to them? How often have you misunderstood what your child was saying?

5. What changes in Jesus does this story seem to best signal?
   ○ A change from the perspective of a child to the perspective of an adult.
   ○ A change from an obedient attitude to a rebellious one.
   ○ A change from dependence to independence.
   ○ A change in who he thought of as his "parent."
   ○ A change from parental direction to self-direction.
   ○ Other_____.

6. How does this story give you comfort or insight?
   ○ Even Jesus' parents had to go through stress and challenges.
   ○ Even Jesus did things that disturbed his parents.
   ○ Developing independence is necessary in growing up.
   ○ Sometimes we misjudge children.
   ○ Sometimes children mature without us really noticing.
   ○ Other_____.

7. How can you help your child to "increase in wisdom" in such a way that will eventually help him or her to be independent?

GOING DEEPER:
If your group has time and/or wants a challenge, go on to these questions.

8. Why do you think this story about Jesus was included in the Bible?

9. How much of Jesus' preparation can be attributed to his godly parents?

Caring Time : 15 min.
APPLY THE LESSON AND PRAY FOR ONE ANOTHER

Leader

Encourage everyone to participate in this important time and be sure that each group member is receiving prayer support. Conclude the prayer time by asking God for guidance in determining the future mission and outreach of this group.

One of the most important things we can do as parents is pray for our children. Take some time now to do just that and to pray for one another. Begin by sharing your responses to the following questions. Then share prayer requests and close in group prayer.

1. What is something you are thankful for about each of your children?

2. What one area of your relationship with your child(ren) needs improvement?

3. How do you most need God's wisdom today in raising your child(ren)?

NEXT WEEK

Today we looked at the joys and frustrations that can come to a marriage when "baby makes three." If even Mary and Joseph needed patience and wisdom in raising Jesus, then how much more do we need to turn to God for help in parenting? In the coming week, pray with your spouse about any concerns regarding your child(ren), and ask the Holy Spirit to help your child(ren) daily to "increase in wisdom and stature, and in favor with God and with people" (v. 52). Next week we will turn to the book of Song of Songs in the Old Testament for guidance in determining the role that sexuality plays in marriage.

NOTES ON LUKE 2:41–52

Summary: This is the only account given in Scripture about the childhood of Jesus. He was a little boy like all others. In this case he showed unusual understanding about the things of God and the Scriptures. The scholars were amazed and Mary, Jesus' mother, took notice. Jesus seemed to be surprised that his parents would not expect him to be talking with the scholars at the Temple.

2:42 When He was 12 years old. At age 13, a Jewish boy was expected to take his place in the religious community of Israel. Age 12 would be a time of preparation for assuming the responsibilities of adulthood. It is unclear whether this was Jesus' first visit to the temple or whether he had accompanied Mary and Joseph on earlier pilgrimages.

2:46 After three days. This does not mean they spent three days in Jerusalem looking for Jesus. Day one was the trip out of the city with the caravan—probably a walk of about 25 miles. Day two was their trip back to the city. Day three was when they found him in the temple. **sitting among the teachers.** It was common for the rabbis to discuss theology in the temple courts. Interested listeners would sit with them and converse about questions that arose from their discussions. **asking them questions.** Even as the Son of God, Jesus had to go through a natural process of learning like every other child. Asking questions was an important part of that learning process.

2:47 all those who heard Him were astounded. This seems to be the first reason why Luke included this story. Jesus' insight into the Law drew the respect and wonder of his elders.

2:48 Mary's response is not amazement at Jesus' insight into the Law, but a motherly one of frustration and concern over Jesus' absence. **Your father and I.** Even though the infant narratives describe Jesus' birth as a virgin birth, Joseph took Jesus as his own child and acted as father to him.

2:49 I must be. Luke records several statements that reflect Jesus' sense of his mission and the steps required to fulfill it (Luke 4:43; 9:22; 24:7). Mary and Joseph's inability to comprehend what he meant is paralleled later on by his family's misunderstanding of him (Luke 8:19–21). **in My Father's interests.** This is the second reason Luke included this story. Mary referred to Joseph as "your father" (v. 48). Jesus' answer to Mary shows his growing realization of his true identity as the Son of God. It may also be a gentle rebuke implying that she should have had this insight as well. The Jews considered the temple to be a place where God was present in a special way.

2:51 was obedient to them. Jesus may have had an awareness he was God's Son, but that didn't keep him from being obedient to his human parents.

2:52 Jesus' growth was not one-dimensional. Some parents really push their children athletically. Others push them musically or in their social or academic development. Often when this happens, the child's development may be advanced in one or two areas and retarded in others. But Jesus grew along several dimensions. He grew physically (in stature). He grew intellectually (in wisdom). He grew socially (in favor with men). But most of all he grew spiritually (in favor with God). The next account of Jesus begins at least 18 years after this event.

Session 6

ONE FLESH

Scripture Song of Songs 1:16; 2:1–7; 4:1–7

 ## LAST WEEK

Mary and Joseph helped us last week look at the challenges we sometimes encounter as parents. We saw their example of providing guidance in the life of Jesus, and how he then "increased in wisdom and stature" (Luke 2:52). We were reminded that discipline is important, but it's also important to take time to listen and to understand what our children are saying. Most of all we need to pray for our children as they deal with the pressures of the world. Today we turn to the important topic of sexuality in marriage.

In this session, we will consider how sex can be maintained. We will also consider sex as a way to find oneness with our partner, instead of becoming something shameful. Marriage is living out a complete personal intimacy that mirrors the intimacy God seeks with all of his children. But at the root of it all is a desire to be one with another person, a drive that is both physical and spiritual. This desire is blessed by God and is good. In Genesis 2:25 we read, "The man and his wife were both naked, and they felt no shame.

 ### Ice Breaker : 15 min.
CONNECT WITH YOUR GROUP

Leader
Begin the session with a word of prayer, asking God for his blessing and presence. Then have each member take turns sharing his or her response to the Ice-Breaker activity.

When was the last time you did something just for the two of you? Take turns responding to the following questions and dream about your ideal getaway. (Don't tell your spouse what you chose and see how different or the same your answers are.)

1. If you had $2,000 to splurge for a second honeymoon, how would you spend it?
   - ○ One glorious weekend in a luxury hotel.
   - ○ One week in a nice hotel.
   - ○ Two weeks sightseeing and staying in economy hotels.
   - ○ Three weeks in the boondocks sleeping in the back of the car.
   - ○ I would save the money.
   - ○ Other_____.

2. If you could take along something to pass the time, what would you take?
   - ○ My laptop computer.
   - ○ My golf clubs.
   - ○ My cell phone.
   - ○ Some good books.
   - ○ My video/DVD collection.
   - ○ Nothing—I'll be too busy.
   - ○ Other_____.

3. With all of this time alone together, what would you talk about the most?
   - ○ Our future.
   - ○ The children.
   - ○ Our spiritual life.
   - ○ Problems at work.
   - ○ Our relationship.
   - ○ Other_____.

 Bible Study : 30 min.
READ SCRIPTURE + DISCUSS

Leader
Ask a couple in the group ahead of time to read aloud the Scripture passage. Have the husband read the words of the "Lover," and the wife read the words of the "Beloved." Then divide into subgroups of three to six for discussion of the Questions for Interaction.

Song of Songs was at one time only looked at as an allegory for Christ's love for the church, but efforts to remove its literal affirmation of human sexual love failed. Famed theologian Karl Barth called the book an extended commentary on Genesis 2:25: *"The man and his wife were both naked, and they felt no shame."* Read Song of Songs 1:16; 2:1–7; 4:1–7 and note how the lovers take care of each other.

A Love Song

Beloved:

[16]How handsome you are, my lover!
Oh, how charming!
And our bed is verdant.

Beloved:

2 I am a rose of Sharon,
a lily of the valleys.

Lover:

[2]Like a lily among thorns
is my darling among the maidens.

Beloved:

[3]Like an apple tree among the trees of the forest
is my lover among the young men.
I delight to sit in his shade,
and his fruit is sweet to my taste.
[4]He has taken me to the banquet hall,
and his banner over me is love.
[5]Strengthen me with raisins,
refresh me with apples,
for I am faint with love.
[6]His left arm is under my head,
and his right arm embraces me.
[7]Daughters of Jerusalem, I charge you
by the gazelles and by the does of the field:
Do not arouse or awaken love
until it so desires.

Lover:

4 How beautiful you are, my darling!
Oh, how beautiful!
Your eyes behind your veil are doves.
Your hair is like a flock of goats
descending from Mount Gilead.
[2]Your teeth are like a flock of sheep just shorn,
coming up from the washing.
Each has its twin;
not one of them is alone.
[3]Your lips are like a scarlet ribbon;
your mouth is lovely.
Your temples behind your veil
are like the halves of a pomegranate.
[4]Your neck is like the tower of David,
built with elegance;
on it hang a thousand shields,
all of them shields of warriors.
[5]Your two breasts are like two fawns,
like twin fawns of a gazelle
that browse among the lilies.
[6]Until the day breaks
and the shadows flee,

*I will go to the mountain of myrrh
and to the hill of incense.
⁷All beautiful you are, my darling;
there is no flaw in you.*

Song of Songs 1:16; 2:1–7; 4:1–7 (NIV)

 # QUESTIONS FOR INTERACTION

Leader

Refer to the Study Notes at the end of this session as needed. If 30 minutes is not enough time to answer all of the questions in this section, conclude the Bible Study by answering question 7. (Be sensitive to the group's preference to discuss some questions only with their spouses.)

1. How do you remember your parents treating the issue of sex when you asked about it?
   - ○ They avoided the subject.
   - ○ They answered every question.
   - ○ They stumbled their way through it.
   - ○ I never asked them.
   - ○ They left it to the school.
   - ○ They left it to the church.
   - ○ They taught me to say "no," but nothing else.
   - ○ Other_____.

2. If you didn't know that this reading was from the Bible, which of the following would you think it was?
   - ○ A love sonnet from the time of Robert and Elizabeth Barrett Browning.
   - ○ Some old love notes we wrote in our first year of marriage.
   - ○ Love notes from two people who had never been married.
   - ○ The script for a movie from the '40s.
   - ○ Words from a tattered page of a book that was passed around in junior high.
   - ○ Other_____.

3. What do you think the woman meant when she said: "Daughters of Jerusalem ... Do not arouse or awaken love until it so desires" (2:7)?

4. Why is friendship an important part of a healthy sexual relationship? How are you and your spouse doing at being best friends?

5. On a scale of 1 ("We never talk about it") to 10 ("We talk about it freely"), how would you rate your ability to discuss sex with your spouse?

6. How are you guarding against marital unfaithfulness? How are you ensuring that neither lovemaking nor friendship is neglected in your marriage? What is the next date on the calendar for just the two of you?

7. What is your biggest challenge or need regarding your sexuality?
   ○ Expressing what my sexual needs are.
   ○ Feeling good about myself.
   ○ Putting my sexual past behind me.
   ○ Feeling the security of being held.
   ○ Being affirmed as an attractive person.
   ○ Controlling my impulses.
   ○ Other_____.

GOING DEEPER:
If your group has time and/or wants a challenge, go on to these questions.

---

8. If God's view of sex in marriage is conveyed here, then why do so many couples experience nothing like it?

9. What do you think the "banner" in 2:4 signifies? How could you apply this to your marriage?

Caring Time : 15 min.
APPLY THE LESSON AND PRAY FOR ONE ANOTHER

Leader
Following the Caring Time, discuss with your group how they would like to celebrate the last session next week. Also, discuss the possibility of splitting into two groups and continuing with another study.

Prayer is a very important way to strengthen the bond between a husband and wife. Begin by responding to the following questions, then share prayer requests and close in prayer.

1. How would you describe your "walk" with Jesus recently?
   ○ Slipping.   ○ Growing.
   ○ Up and down.   ○ Other_____
   ○ Very close.

2. In what ways has your spouse been a blessing to you this past week?

3. What positive step can you take this week to insure time and privacy to nurture your love life?

 **NEXT WEEK**

Today we looked at the important matter of sexuality in marriage. We were reminded by the beautiful passage in Song of Songs that God created sex as a wonderful experience that brings both pleasure and intimacy. It's only when sex is used as a way of focusing on self and selfish physical need that it becomes shameful. In the coming week, be sure to express your love for your spouse in some way every day, whether it be through compliments, notes, little gifts, an unexpected phone call, etc. Be creative! In our next and final session we will talk about commitment and what mature love is all about.

 NOTES ON SONG OF SONGS 1:16; 2:1-7; 4:1-7

2:1-2 a lily among thorns. Referring to the beloved's self-description in verse 1, the lover compares her favorably to the court maidens.

2:4 banner. The king boldly displays his love for all to see, like the large flag identifying military forces. Even today Jewish weddings are held under a banner or covering. The banner imagery is repeated in 6:4 as a battle flag (Num. 2:2; Ps. 20:5).

2:5-6 A poetic description of joyful, marital sexual love. **raisins ... apples.** These are symbols of sexual passion in the ancient Near East.

2:7 The beloved repeats this refrain (3:5; 5:8; 8:4), while describing her physical pleasure with the king. **gazelle ... does.** These beautiful and graceful animals serve as witnesses to the beloved's charge—a picture that fits well with the writer's many imaginative references to nature in the Song. **until it so desires.** The beloved has

learned a lesson from her love life: Don't force love or manipulate it. Instead, avoid premarital physical relations and let love be open, spontaneous at its own pace.

4:1 eyes behind your veil. A veil may cover the beloved's face, but the lover still sees the beauty underneath, as well as in her eyes. **a flock of goats descending.** Goats common in Canaan were generally black; the lover sees his beloved's dark hair cascading down.

4:2 sheep just shorn. The sheep would thus have been clean and white.

4:3 Your lips ... scarlet. Egyptian women often painted their lips, so perhaps the beloved followed their example.

4:4 Your neck is like the tower. Her neck, adorned with beautiful necklaces, was long, strong and straight.

4:5 two fawns. Fawns are young, sweet, delicate and not fully-grown. 4:6 Until the day breaks. Their wedding night was long and passionate.

Session 7
TILL DEATH DO US PART
Scripture 1 Corinthians 13:1–7

 **LAST WEEK**

We looked to the Song of Songs last week to help us understand how God views sexuality within the marriage relationship. We were reminded that it mirrors the intimacy God seeks with all of his children. Although the world has turned sex into something shameful and selfish, it is a wonderful experience in marriage, and is a way to strengthen and find oneness in that relationship. Because of its importance, we need to find the time and privacy to nurture our love life. Today we will talk about the importance of commitment within marriage.

Commitment has become a rather difficult issue today, especially among "baby boomers." Divorce has hit epidemic proportions—it seems like every life has been touched in some way by divorce. If something doesn't change, the couple who actually lives up to the vow "till death do us part" will become the exception rather than the rule.

Part of the problem seems to be that we live in a "What's in it for me?" culture. Once marriage becomes a situation where the "profit-loss" balance sheet no longer seems to be "in the black," some feel it's time to bail out as if they were selling a falling stock.

Whether divorce should ever really be an option for Christians could probably be debated for a long time. But it's clear that God's intent is for marriage to be "till death do us part." Such commitment to each other is scriptural. And it also gives people a sense of security, knowing that marriage is a relationship on which they can rely.

Ice-Breaker : 15 min.
CONNECT WITH YOUR GROUP

Leader

Begin this final session with a word of prayer and thanksgiving for this time together. Be sure to affirm each couple for the blessings and contributions that they made to the group.

What have you learned about yourself and your marriage while being with this group? Together as a couple, pick one of the following "houses" or make up your own to describe how this group has helped you.

○ SLEEPING BAG FOR TWO: Because you have helped us to get back to the simple things, a simple lifestyle—wide open to the outdoors, the stars, smelling the flowers and listening to the birds again.

○ GLASS HOUSE: Because you have allowed us to be open and free—to look at the world around, get rid of our rocks and enjoy life—to let the sun shine in.

○ SWISS FAMILY ROBINSON TREE HOUSE: Because you have helped us to rebuild our family, work together, see the inner strength in each other and accept the situation as a new challenge.

○ GREENWICH VILLAGE APARTMENT: Because you helped us to know each other, to be ourselves, to celebrate the "wild, way-out" side of each other, to care less about conformity and "measuring up" to others' expectations.

○ LOG CABIN: Because you have affirmed our pioneering spirit that strikes out into unknown expeditions, "homesteading" new frontiers in our spiritual journey.

○ WINNEBAGO CRUISER: Because you have released in us a desire to travel the "back roads" and to rediscover our heritage—the old watering holes of our childhood and the simple joys of life.

○ EIGHT-PERSON TENT: Because we want to share more of us with the rest of you. We have become a family together, and there is so much more we can share.

○ HOUSEBOAT: Because you have started us on a cruise into uncharted waters and new adventures ... and we would like you to share the adventure with us. The pace will be slower and the facilities a little crowded, but you are all welcome.

○ PORTABLE SANDBOX: Because you have helped us to discover a child inside that we didn't know was there; the party is just beginning.

○ TRAVELING CIRCUS TRAIN: Because you have said it's okay to laugh in the midst of pain, rejoice when times are tough and celebrate life in all its fullness.

○ OTHER:_____.

 Bible Study : 30 min.
READ SCRIPTURE ✦ DISCUSS

Leader
Select a member of the group ahead of time to read aloud the Scripture passage. Then discuss the Questions for Interaction, breaking up into smaller groups of three to six.

In this soaring hymn of praise to love (which has become a classic piece of literature), Paul points out the primacy of love and describes what love does and does not do. He defines love in terms of action and attitude. Read 1 Corinthians 13:1–7 and note what Paul means by "an even better way" (1 Cor. 12:31).

Love

13 *If I speak the languages of men and of angels,*
but do not have love,
I am a sounding gong or a clanging cymbal.
²If I have the gift of prophecy,
and understand all mysteries and all knowledge,
and if I have all faith, so that I can move mountains,
but do not have love,
I am nothing.
³And if I donate all my goods to feed the poor,
and if I give my body to be burned,
but do not have love,
I gain nothing.
⁴Love is patient; love is kind. Love does not envy;
is not boastful; is not conceited;
⁵does not act improperly; is not selfish;
is not provoked; does not keep a record of wrongs;
⁶finds no joy in unrighteousness, but rejoices in the truth;
⁷bears all things, believes all things,
hopes all things, endures all things.

1 Corinthians 13:1–7

QUESTIONS FOR INTERACTION

Leader

Refer to the Study Notes at the end of this session as needed. If 30 minutes is not enough time to answer all of the questions in this section, conclude the Bible Study by answering questions 6 and 7.

1. What is your favorite love song, poem or romantic movie?

2. How easy is it to tell your spouse of your love? Choose one of the following that expreses your situation.
   ○ It's hard because I never heard "I love you" when I was growing up.
   ○ It doesn't come naturally, but I'm trying.
   ○ It's easy for me, but sometimes I forget.
   ○ I don't need to tell my spouse, because it goes without saying.
   ○ Other_____.

3. Why is love more important than eloquent speech, superior knowledge and sacrificial giving?

4. Looking at the descriptions of perfect love in verses 4-7, in which one of these descriptions are you strongest? In which one are you weakest?

5. How would your marriage be different if you could practice this kind of love every day?

6. Thinking about all of the aspects of marriage that we have discussed throughout this course, take turns answering true or false to the following statements and explain why you chose that answer.
   ○ A strong marriage relationship, once broken, is very difficult to restore.
   ○ A marriage must change over time if it is to survive.
   ○ Marriage can supply all of our relationship needs.
   ○ A marriage can be good without being intimate.
   ○ Men more than women lose their identity in a marriage relationship.

7. What would help you to have the marriage that God desires?

8. How does love as described in this chapter compare to love as typically defined in our culture?

9. What would Jesus say is necessary for a couple to have a fulfilling, solid marriage?

 Caring Time : 15 min.

APPLY THE LESSON AND PRAY FOR ONE ANOTHER

Leader
Conclude this final Caring Time by praying for each couple and asking for God's blessing in any plans to start a new group and/or continue to study together.

Gather around each other now in this final time of sharing and prayer and give each other the support needed to trust that God will work to strengthen and bless your marriage in the years to come.

1. How has this group been a blessing in your life?

2. During this course, what are some specific areas in which you have strengthened your marriage?
   ○ Handling pressures and making our marriage a top priority.
   ○ Understanding each other and constructively handling our differences.
   ○ Appreciating our past and learning from the hard times.
   ○ Relating to our children and extended families.
   ○ Making sex and romance an integral part of our marriage.
   ○ Affirming regularly our lasting commitment to each other.
   ○ Other_____.

3. What is something you can do in the coming weeks to affirm your commitment to your spouse and your marriage?

WHAT'S NEXT?

Today Paul reminded us, in very practical terms, of what love is and what it is not. He shared that if love is not present, then nothing else has any significance. When we look at Paul's words in terms of our marriage, then we can evaluate and see how to improve the love we have for our spouse. In the weeks ahead, go back and read this passage often to find new and different ways in which you can make love your number one priority.

NOTES ON I CORINTHIANS 13:1-7

Summary: This classic passage about love falls within a section about division within the church. Paul is calling attention to the need for the individual to support the good of the whole. All believers are to exercise their individual gifts with love for the unity of the body in the bond of peace. The opposite happens when an individual calls attention to himself or acts to the determent of others. This description of Christian love puts the other person first. This is especially true within the marriage. If the husband or wife does not seek the good of the spouse first, then conflict will certainly follow.

13:1 the languages of men and of angels. Ecstatic speech—highly prized in Corinth—is an authentic gift of the Holy Spirit. However, it becomes like the unintelligible noise of pagan worship when used outside the context of love. **gong / cymbal.** Paul is probably thinking of the repetitious and meaningless noise generated at pagan temples by beating on metal instruments.

13:2 Paul contrasts three other spiritual gifts with love: prophecy, knowledge and faith. **prophecy.** Such activity is highly commended by Paul (14:1), yet without love a prophet is really nothing. **understand all mysteries.** In Corinth, special and esoteric knowledge was highly valued (1:18–2:16); but even if one knew the very secrets of God, without love it would be to no end. That which makes a person significant (i.e., the opposite of "nothing") is not a gift like prophecy or knowledge, but the ability to love. **faith, so that I can move mountains.** Paul refers to Jesus' words in Mark 11:23—even such massive faith that can unleash God's power in visible ways is not enough to make a person significant without love at its foundation.

13:3 donate all my goods to feed

the poor. Presumably Paul refers to goods and property given to others, but not in love. The point is not: do not give if you cannot do so in love (the poor still profit from gifts, regardless of the spirit in which they are given), but rather that the loveless giver gains no reward on the Day of Judgment. **give my body.** Not even martyrdom—giving up one's life for the sake of another or in a great cause—brings personal benefit when it is done outside love.

13:4 patient. This word describes patience with people (not circumstances). It characterizes the person who is slow to anger (long-suffering) despite provocation. **kind.** The loving person does good to others. not envy. The loving person does not covet what others have, nor begrudge them their possessions. **not boastful.** The loving person is self-effacing, not a braggart. **not conceited**. Literally, not "puffed up." The loving person does not need others to feel inferior, nor looks down on people.

13:5 does not act improperly. The same Greek word is used in 7:36 to describe a man who led on a woman, but then refused to marry her. **not selfish.** Loving people not only do not insist on their rights, but will give up their due for the sake of others. **not provoked.** Other people do not easily anger loving people; they are not touchy. **does not keep a record of wrongs.** The verb is an accounting term, and the image is of a ledger sheet on which wrongs received are recorded. The loving person forgives and forgets.

13:6 finds no joy in unrighteousness. Loving people do not rejoice when others fail (which could make them feel superior), nor enjoy pointing out the wrong in others. **rejoices in the truth.** Paul shifts back to the positive.

13:7 believes. Love never loses faith. **hopes.** Love continually looks forward. **endures.** Love keeps loving despite hardship.

PERSONAL NOTES